Sunbathing with Fishermen

by

Penny Sharman

First published 2024 by The Hedgehog Poetry Press,

5 Coppack House, Churchill Avenue, Clevedon. BS21 6QW

www.hedgehogpress.co.uk

ISBN: 978-1-916830-35-6

I dedicate this book
with love

to my brother

John Sharman
24.4.51-6.2021

Even though
we didn't talk much,
I miss his presence daily

This is very much a collection about growing up in the 50's and 60's and how becoming pregnant as a teenager and being sent away from home to an unmarried mother and baby home has affected my whole life. The collection includes poems from the Cotswolds, Oxford, Manchester and the Pennines. It includes themes such as love and loss of family, lovers and friends. As I have just turned seventy-five, I very much consider this collection a reverie, looking back and taking stock, going forward to my crone stage as a woman. Of course, there are poems about the pandemic and coming to terms with grief. I am always inspired to write by the natural landscape and many of these poems will reflect this in the imagery and metaphors.

Contents

IN THIS WILDERNESS
OF WANT AND NEED,
FIRST STEPS, THE
ONE ALONE WHO HOLDS
HANDS WITH CHANGE
WILL LANDSCAPE
OUR FUTURE

BURFORD CHURCH

I can't remember my long white gown,
or the handmade lace around the hem,
the family heirloom worn by generations
of tiny fingers and toes.

I can't remember the vaulted ceiling, or carved
figures of John the Baptist, or Saint Catherine
holding her wheel. I didn't smell the baptism oil
in the aumbry cupboard.

I can't remember Anthony Sedley`s
etched plea on the font or the boom
of Cromwell's voice yelling at the Levellers.

I can't remember the holy water splashing
over my forehead or old faces staring at new life.
But I must have seen the vicar`s mouth move.

I must have heard my own wailing tongue,
licked the blessings on my lips, kicked my feet
on the ancient stone font. I will have smelt
the 4711 on mum`s tender skin.

INGREDIENTS FROM THE HIGH STREET

I arrived in the kitchen
lived on squares of yellow and orange linoleum
I squealed a lot
I grew long legs and ran around the larder
felt the cold stone slab in the palms of my tiny hands
thought about dancing
mum dressed me in skirts covered in cockleshells
I wore blue ribbons in my hair
I grew big eyes and red lips
I kissed lots of boys
I believed love was
Cadbury's chocolate and the smell of leather shoes
I grew babies inside myself
one two three   they squealed a lot
and did naughty things
I never ran away from the kitchen
I was always young
I baked cakes and strudels
I loved to look out of the windows
where sky was blue
grass was red and never cut
where runner beans
never stopped climbing
I danced so much my feet grew wings
I levitated the top of my head reached the ceiling of house
where white was magnolia
like a lullaby it kept me cooking rabbit stew
and nut roast
I became a professor of gravy
there were days and years
where a mother and father
sent me away from the mystery
of shame and puddings
there were days and years
I came home in a pushchair
I had roller skate shoes when doors blew open
pianos played Mozart I felt wind in my hair

FIRST DAY

small everything about me small hands feet legs arms tears and the newness of leather shoes white blouse pleated skirt a blue ribbon in my hair everything small about me mum holding my hand a skip on the cobbles black bumps down the high street monsters under the grids the builder's yard sawdust pine perfume the bakers yeast filled air small voices the noise of happy the noise of sad the witch in the sweet shop everything big at the gates iron padlocks rust tarmac spiked railings mum and me everything quiet in rooms boggarts in the cupboards blackboards chalk children in bubbles whispers in the desks caterpillars' in the cabbage giant spiders in the toilets everything big air above the school angels flying over roofs that first day mum me the instant of aloneness

OUTDOOR SWIMMING POOL

Filkins 1958

This is
where I became buoyant
lost the rubber tyre and
nothing could stop me in the green water,
round and round I swam to freedom
with a lightness of an angel's wings.

This is
where I bared my flesh
each spring and summer
to wind, rain and sunshine.
I led a goose-pimpled life
as I gulped in cold water.

This is
where I heard stories of whales,
dolphins, mermaids, the kraken,
where I breathed in blue water
and never thought of drowning
or the dark bottom of oceans.

This is
where I laughed, lived in my small world
of safety in the pool, playgrounds,
maypole dancing and mum's soft skin.
Each night I checked the wardrobe
and under the bed for monsters.

This is
where winter ice froze out a normal life,
gifted me with icicles outside of windows.
whiteouts and Jack's artwork on glass
a comfort as I sat by coal fires
with a toasting fork and crumpets,
outdoor swimming lost to dreams.

RIVER WINDRUSH: A CHILD'S SWIMMING DAYS

So it goes, constantly, the river's meandering.
Wild swimming is a trend today, as if we never did
slip into our own river in the 50's, as if it was never
the natural way for our feet to be drawn to water.

Let's go swimming on the bend where the river bank
is thick orange mud that squeezes between our toes,
where Dace and Grayling see us coming: where
Crayfish once bit our legs. Let's wrap our cossies
in a towel, be naked in the elements, feel goosebumps
on our buttocks and breasts. Let's talk to the black
and white cows, whisper secrets to weeping willows.

So it goes, constantly, the river's meandering.
The dark spinning black glass of the whirlpool,
stories of being taken by a whirlpool force, down
to a bottomless grave.

We can still wonder again at the Oxbow Lake,
the meaning of being alone, cut off, adrift from
the main stream where we learnt to tie shoe laces
with a finger and thumb, the drudgery of beeswax
polishing, the dusting of men and babies.

Let's recall the freedom of swimming with wildness
in our hinterland, in water meadows that flood with ease,
the coming and going of wetness like breathing in and out.
Constantly, so it goes, the meandering of our river.

THE BUGHOUSE

It's still there, the tall building with an ochre face,
tombstone bricks that stare out to the world.
The top of the house higher than the lime trees
in the street, small windows under roof tops with
eyes that blink in sun-light, weep in rain.

The locals said it was full of ghosts, full of secrets.

What I remember most is the climb up splintered
wooden steps in the dark, sitting in silence, waiting,
waiting for that one single shaft of light from
a projector's turning eye:

a flash of a white face, black velvet hair,
ruby lips in Technicolor, a whistled tune, blue birds
that danced through open windows, my heart beating fast
when her teeth bit into the apple.

SUNBATHING WITH FISHERMEN

We're the girls sitting on the riverbank by Radcot Bridge.
We're the girls watching red and yellow floats bob up and down.

Mum brings out the cheese and tomato sandwiches,
peels shell off the hard-boiled eggs.

We're the girls in our bikinis thinking of swimming
with the perch, dace and minnows, but not moving
as something called quiet is needed for the eyes of men
watching the line for the slightest bite, for the slightest bite.

We're the girls– me, Christine and Susan thinking
about boys, wondering about the blood thing and how
many babies we might have.

We're the girls watching my Aunty Marg fish with the men,
hear her laugh when she banks a fat eel.

We're the girls lying on the blanket watching,
such a wonder in our eyes.

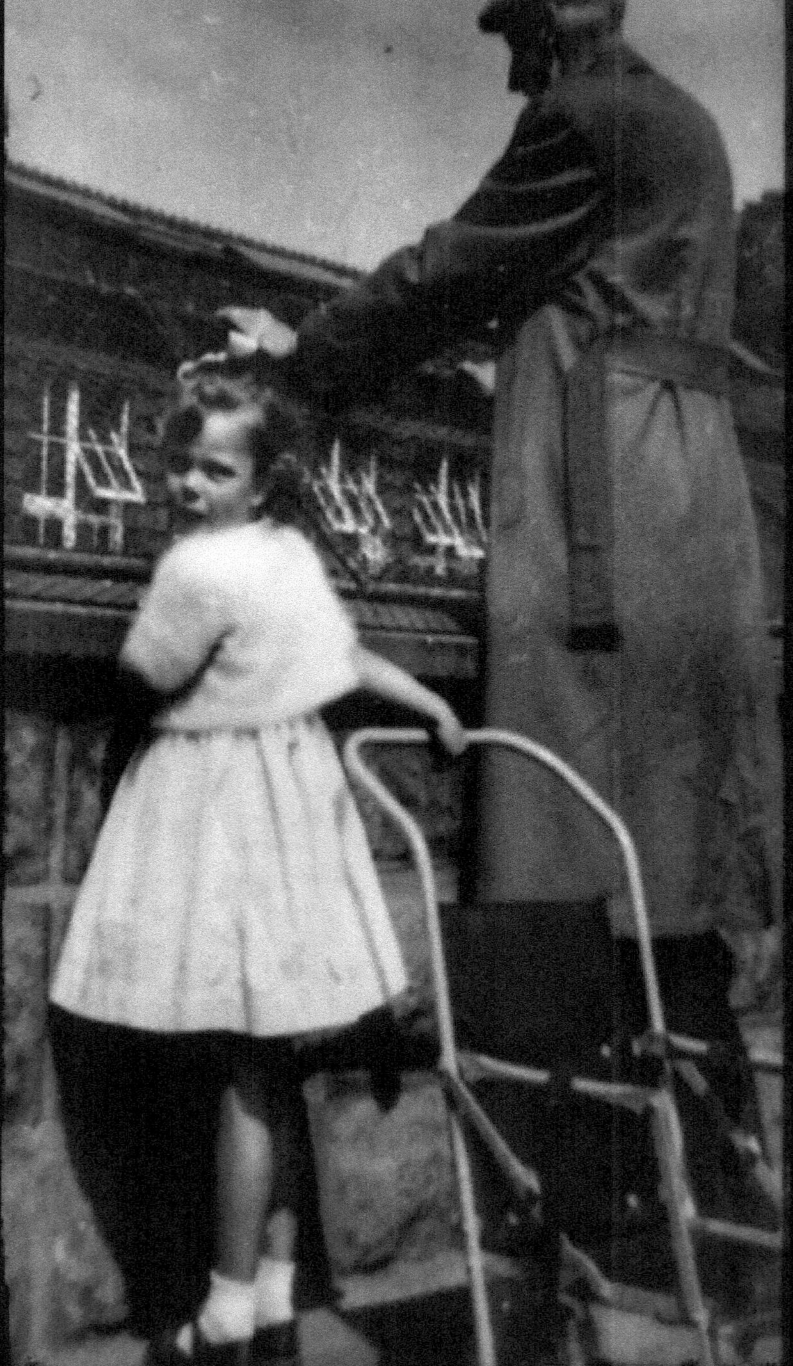

MAYPOLE

those rainbow ribbons
twisting above our heads
over and under
under and over
the joy the whole sky
coming at you smiling
heads up
heads down
arms and feet moving over grass
dancing on tarmac
sometimes doing it right
sometimes doing it un-right
but mostly it was
a roller coaster of fun

then there was the music
for the first time
the music

WATCHING DAD AND AUNTY MARG FISH NEAR RADCOT BRIDGE, 1958

I never had a hankering for catching fish,
to follow a family tradition of hook and line,
wet stale bread squeezed into a tight ball,
to bait the innocent scaled creatures.
But I loved to watch Dad and Marg laugh,
take a drag on their cigarettes,
some holy communion between siblings.

I never nurtured the gall to hold a dying
cold fish, a silver beauty in my palms,
or try to prize out the barb from its
gawp of fear. I could hear dad egging me on,
but all I could say was
it must really hurt the fish dad.

Each time I was relieved when dad
put the fish back in the river, watched
the Rudd, Perch, Roach and Dace swim away
from dad and me, land monsters on a river bank.

CRADLE

I come from the bog sedge,
cotton candy, hair tassels that dance;
a flower to take your breath away.
I come from our pillow talk,
you and me ageing in a bed of stories;

I am seed and stem, wide-open spaces,
the sky and stars. I come from the music,
violins and voices, marching melodies.
From granddads wood shavings, his chisel and chip knife;
where heartbreaks hide in the rings of trees.
I come from water, the outdoor pool,
green water where I learnt to float, the deep end,
my eyes sore from chlorine.

I come from the sea; salt encrusted in wounds.
I come from a need to belong, my memories
of abandonment. I come from purple and pink,
columbine in my garden, by the roadside,
my delicate petals, my dancing spires in April's breeze.

I come from the May-time, the greening where
flesh is plump, lips wet with dew cups.
Fecund; I am ready; I wait for a garland for my hair.

MUSEUM OF DANCING

Unformed toes in a foetal sac
the twitch to a mother's quickstep and tango

a girl's soft skin in pink leather ballet shoes
a wish for a blue net tutu skirt

a schoolgirl's dance in the playground
hopscotch   jumping a rope   the air
the ability to twirl like Isadora
feel sand between her toes

a teenage fix when head banging
and toe tapping synchronise
the knowledge of who you are

the persistence to go barefoot on wooden floors
where earth is a drum beat to a skeleton
where trampoline is music

a mother's way of soothing
a child's misery to sleep
the sway-sway of her hips

a wise woman's need for twirling
dervishing her rhythm under skin
over and over and over again

ODE TO UTERUS

Oh, pear shaped sea monster
centre of me
how you have taught me
to be woman
given me timed blood
lethal cramps insightful days
nightmare nights

Oh, small closet
inside of me
how you expand
wealth of new life
stretch yourself
unfathomable balloon

Oh, sensible entity
how you rid me
of imperfection
streams of red deltas
down my inner thighs
how your clock knows
more than I will ever know

Oh, fallopian brain
splayed hands
gatherer of seeds
how you tingle inside
give hope to cradles

ICE-FLOWER

I became an ice-flower, my girl's heart frozen,
hard petals in a cage. A fragile beauty walked with
my days of exile. But I held on like the bird's-eye primrose.
I captured her yellow, her intense eye that glows
at the heart of each flower.

I held on to purple from the Teesdale violets,
smallest of treasures for abandoned thought. I hung on
to sunshine and sugared limestone.

The great Whin Sill herself did not let me fall.
She held my feet steady, my boy beating in my womb.
I bathed in the royal blue of early spring gentians,
survivors from an ice-age.

Secrets   Secrets   Secrets   we were   Secrets

I grasped each flower to my heart until the melt,
one by one the ice floes told me I was right, that it
was safe to return to summer.

Each petal from my ice-flower heart dripped away
a rhythm to my dance on the hillside, it captured my
waving and twirling, love for a whole world to see,
my baby at my breast.

MOTHER AND BABY HOME 1967

I've been trying to tell you for years about my mother's suitcase.
I have no memory of packing it. She must have put in my dresses
and jeans, my favourite pyjamas, my white cotton socks.

She must have locked it tight. It will have been put in the car boot,
travelled far away from home, carried up two flights of stairs
and emptied into a cupboard. I have no memory of such an action.
All the other girls were already there, waiting, just waiting.

There was a girl called Susan, she'd seen my luggage;
a mini skirt that cried, a notebook full of writing
that said *are you okay?* My mother's dancing shoes,
her warm skin, two vermillion lipsticks that had lost
the knowledge of speech.

She said she had seen the face of my dad stuck in the corner
of the case; his tweed jacket very comfortable on his shoulders.
She mentioned a worn brown teddy bear, said it looked lost.

She wondered about the small cage that held a mobile of a
beating heart. She described a photograph of my baby brother
shuffling on his bottom; I do remember he never crawled.

She even heard blackbirds singing in a faraway garden,
saw a fallen egg, pale blue and mottled, an undiscovered galaxy.
I have no memory of my suitcase, of lost luggage days.

CUCKOOFLOWER

Keep me close to water,
call me what you will,
milkmaid or a lady's-smock.
I'm a dreamer in the meadows,
pretty pale violet pink,
a delicate hairless beauty,
a bitter cress to chew.

Keep me close to water,
free in the outside air,
do not bring me indoors,
do not tether me in a May's
wedding garland, let me hear
the wind blow sadness away,
let me dance with queen Mab,
hear the cuckoo's song.

MILKWORT

Sisters of mercy

They made us drink eight bottles of water a day to make milk
for the babies, but my coat of many colours could only stomach
two as I prayed for cups of tea and nipples that wouldn't crack.

They made us wash the outside of windows with cold water
and ripped up news, shine the front steps with Cardinal red tile polish.
Two by two we went to Sunday service; two by two we walked
down and up the long hill, a rogation of girls.

They didn't smile much or hold anyone's hand; they were
good at gas and air, good at stitching flesh back together.
They were trained to take away your baby, leave you alone
to dream of a new life.

MARRIAGE BED

Apple pie corners
trap the way you bullied
do you think about
the first time you
hit me around the face
black eye scared heart
how the baby cried
or how you bellowed
at the dinner table
can you pray in your coffin for forgiveness
my boys still in short trousers and innocence
how you made them eat soap
stand in the corner
sit with their hands on their heads
to make you feel big.
Bully Boy.
Sick Man.
Do you turn in your grave?
Remember when
you lied a hundred times
stole my babies' money   or
when you chucked my
clothes out of the window
frightened my mum
threatened to blow up the house.
Bully Boy.
Sick man.
Or that day you held me down
your sweaty palm over my mouth?

Well, do you?
Do you recall
Heaven's Gate
when we all ran
fast as cheetahs
far away from the hunt.

FALSE SEDGE

Bog Sedge

Between hard rock and this constant mountain spring,
a glacier's speed, here are the sorrows.

I shake my hair, wild petals,
sepia notions of common sense
to a marriage bed where hope
is isolated, is abandoned grass.

Where my babies hate
this surrogate daddy,
who makes them eat soap,
sits them down like statues,
scowls into their night of dreams.

He scares the stalk of me with his devil's mind,
hits with his bony fist, penetrates the sap of me.

Oh false sedge, bog sedge,
no sense in any wildflower,
all that's left now is rare
in Teesdale's high hills.

MOONWORT

Alchemy of the mind

There's more magic in me than I know what to do with. Tribe after tribe would come and find me in a moon-charged dewy midnight. I was prized for my spell worthiness; my green leaves, my image of moon mother. My story is made up of superstition, monsters under the bed and sheets that covered up your fears. You believe I can protect you from the mysteries out there in space. You think I will pull out your memories of hurt, the special ones where he chased you around the house with a large knife and locked you in the cupboard, or that time he took your baby into the bedroom and threatened to blow up the camping stove, or that time he made your boys eat soap, or that time he made you all sit on the floor with your hands on your heads. If only you'd had my potion then. If only you'd possessed such a moon magic.

AFTER HE'D GONE

she closed the door like a pillowcase full of feathers.
The Yale lock slipped like oil into its home.
She became a statue, remembered to breathe in and out,
shook her dragon head. Relief became her own tsunami.

She picked up her medicine drum, stroked the elk hide,
knew she was ready to beat a steady rhythm into every
room, each corner filled with his dust, dead skin memories.
She burnt sweet grass to cleanse him from her floorboards,

duvet, toilet bowl, kitchen sink and cutlery. She moved furniture
and hoovered up his claustrophobic fingers. She danced to Frank
Zappa and Ry Cooper, squashed his jealousies and demands
under her toes, she blew them out of windows with puffed cheeks.

She lay down on carpets, turned herself over and over, a whirlwind
of happy grief. She screamed at the bed bugs and curtain moths until
her world turned green and blue. She turned on taps and flooded
the stairway, made rivers gush out of every door.

She made a tabletop raft; her dresses became sails. She waved
goodbye to walls and gardens, felt cold black water in her blood.
She sailed beyond front gardens and cul-de-sac life, park and
playground. She rode a free wave forever.

FINDING HOME
WHERE A
HEART
CAN SETTLE

THE SCHOOL CLOCK

We rescued the school clock
knowing that a breath
was captured in its hands.

We rubbed thick beeswax
into the oak grain, the casement
that held a memory of rhythm.

In-between its bones, the cogs
and jaws of synchronicity bled
with golden oils from a Pharaoh's tomb.

Roman hands reclaimed the buried
motion of planets and stars, the daily
routine of clicking grasshoppers.

It begins with a brass key and
eagle's wings, a swish of a pendulum,
a re-winding of hearts.

Like that night when we stood still
on John Dalton Street staring up, holding on
with our feet as our planet was spinning fast.

SUNRISE

she says
        the charcoal on paper
        maybe a kiss
        it`s thick paper
        red and orange
        a streak
        a lingering
        from the Texas plains

she says
        you can hear it all
        like the ocean
        the blue green music
        look at them
        sound waves
        brush strokes
        ripples
        the edges of love

TO SHRIVE

To the pebble on the windowsill inscribed with love
I whisper the lies I tell myself about being forsaken by friends.

To the stuffed elephants made from recycled sari silks
from Kolkata I sing harmonies to all my graveyards, memories
of truth and kindness.

To the hand-turned wooden mushroom made for darning
holes in socks I tell stories about the hardened arteries inside
my flesh and bone, the sadness.

To the forties mouth-blown glass obsolete red and gold ashtray
I choke on my thoughts of losing a mother and father,
words unspoken.

To the upright hawthorn talking stick resting on my bedroom
wall I give my secret wishes for forgiveness, for a softness
to return to days.

To the screwdrivers and pencils standing alone in a porcelain
Mug I confess my wildness of nature, my mouth and eyes
that scream.

To the green-man-rattle made from oak and cow bladder
on my alter I offer up a prayer for moving on from this fat
Tuesday, a quilted-heart.

To abstract notions of abandonment that lies down
in every cell I give up chocolate, booze, shopping madness, focus
on my gifts within.

PRACTICAL LESSONS IN HYPNOTISM

Never close your eyes when stirring stew on the hob,
like that time when you believed the boy you loved
was true, when he lifted up your skirt in the ginnel
by Burford Church; even when the clock-tower struck
ten you were suckered into his world of want. Maybe
you were a Cinderella, but now you are more.

Always cut your own fringe so that the way is clear,
forget about the Kathy McGowan look of the sixties,
or this present-day trend to hide your eyes from view.
Vision is a necessity to find a way through the maze of men.
You do remember don't you about that man who pulled
down the stars for you, then punched you in the face?

It's not about the crystal pendant swung in front of your eyes,
the sway-sway of his rhythmic hips, that malarky on dance-floors,
how a boys' lips are wine, their soft skin a drug in a kissing bed.
Remember that day when the man gagged you, beasted
the breath from you, when you never knew it was coming?
It's about being savvy, being a queen of the rumba.

TO WRITE A LOVE LETTER IS MORE THAN A DAY'S WORK

It's alchemical
moving one life towards another,
finding the turning point,
the spectrum of words for longing hearts.

It's about handmade paper
from pulped rags, the shredding
of syllables and patience,
the boiling and washing, to find
a white page for scribing love.

It's about the flight from
a goose's wing feather plucked
from its daily chores. It's about
the sharp blade that whittles a point.
It's about cleaning the hollow shaft
of its quick so that liquid love can flow.

It's about the iron gall,
borrowing from oak and wasp,
the molecules and tannins, a symbiosis
of salts and sulphate, gum Arabic,
sticky blood love, ink that conjures
sighs and kisses from the air.

OILSKIN COAT

Mine shone like black patent leather.
It was long and the belt fixed me into the 60's,
a Cathy McGowan copy, everything Mod,
long hair, tartan maxi skirt, with a heart
that thought life was as simple as baking
a victoria sponge.

My recipe left out the ingredients and method.
All the sifting I had to do between sheets
and duvets, hennaed hair and kaftans, the
folding in of salted tears and placentas
to find the perfect dropping consistency for love.

You tell me again, how often we were in
the same road, town or concert hall over time,
and never recognised our future–how close
we were to holding hands when I wore
my oilskin coat and knee high boots.

ON MAGDALEN BRIDGE

Sky is dark blue and starlight throws light
on the Cherwell. Punts dream of wild days,
their movement through deep waters.

Dark sky hears the wooden punts make music.
They knock into each other against the river's flow,
and all I can think about is falling.

I fall overboard. I fall for you. You laugh to see
me soaked; my dress shrunk. I am bone cold on
Magdalen Bridge, stars wait to shine on blue water.

Starlight falls over Magdalen Tower. The icon.
The sky is cerulean. Choirboys are ready to sing
in the May, I'm ready to jump into dirty water.

The light appears as dark blue fades and so many
of us sing with red wine lips. This is the day of days,
music of generations, joy of another hug with you.

Sky is baby blue and birdsong; we are bells on toes,
hawthorn blossom hair, and all I think about is falling,
falling overboard, backwards towards you.

THE SEA KNIFE

with you I could cut up words
sharpen crab shells
walrus tusks
limpet homes
there's a roughness to any edge
of quill or heart there's a deep wound
from mouths that whisper lies
with you I could cut up
bladderwrack and dulse
turn their ribbons
weave a shadow cloak
with you I could fish
in any chalk ocean
find all my new words
my alien language.

SCAPEGOAT

after Holman Hunt

i wanted to give you the rainbow
that spans the hills
sees the desert
hears sand move
over bones of our ancestors

i wanted to tell you stories
about the animal
how light illuminates
his aloneness
how he's blamed
for everything

how his eyes
reach out to me
full of sadness
with violet and indigo
hope in the grit
smallest of rocks
on a dry valley floor
i wanted to give you the colour

ENDYMION

If I was her, goddess of moonlight,
it might explain the light, the blue,
how she casts such a spell, hypnotic fields,
the exact way I feel about you.

If I was her, I'd trap you in time,
bell on bell, songs again in dusk,
in dawn's day over, nights under
you, tall trees, ships through the years.

SEARCHING FOR A RING TONE

If you press button A
I'll be able to hear your voice.
All those words from pen to paper.
I'll imagine your tongue, red lips,
your hot blood, the pump of you.

If you press button A
it will all make sense, the scriptures
and texts sent from a survivor
of broken hearts, our search into
knuckle and bone, all those years
of mirror gazing.

If you would only press button A
in that red obsolete box
stuck in a country lane
I'd smell your messages
of vinegar and brown paper,
your ripped directory of love.

If you could press button A
by some fluke of Aphrodite's hand,
magnetise us together for good,
then the numbers might sigh a relief,
the stars above you might say
maybe, yes, maybe.

THE WILDERNESS DAYS

There is something quite strange about awakening in April.
Yesterday, in that other month, all was easy, calm, but nothing is
today. I cannot reach you by any machinery. I could try the
other way, the old way, read your mind, but this is the cruellest
dagger; how to deal with thoughts of you in that other month.

When I close my eyes, years pass backwards, a baby you, me breeding,
breeding you once more like the tiny-tiny buds growing on lilacs.
When I breathe in tomorrow's air will your puzzle unfold out
into some new truth, not this misery that I'm dreaming of?
This clock is too long, the hours, buckets full of worry, the

ticking hand speaks constantly, a metronome in my dead
heart. Will you come soon; relieve my rubbing palms, this land
of unknowing if you are well in your mind. Maybe I'm mixing
too many seeds in this pot of ideas, this flowery bed of memory.
How I question the smell of your unwashed hair, dirty hands and

how light and airy days were in March, the quantity of desire.
But with waking I am filled with a nag like bluebottles stirring,
hungry for the taste of you on my cheeks, not this dull, dull
Tuesday in a day that knows nothing more than a tangle of roots,
photographs of a homecoming, a hug of you, a kiss-kiss with

my boyish you, my happy you, carefree, pocket full of spring.
Today is still strange, curtains hold back day, hold out the rain.

WDIG COTTAGE

Out here today
nothing but sky
and towering cumulus
ladders to the stars
movement a troll's pace.

Out here today
heat, sharp sunshine
sloth legs in boots
and all that life
in the stubble fields,

hare   bullfinch   beetle
peacock   butterfly   crow
buzzards that circle the hearth,
those late dragonflies.

Out here today
the will, the want to
walk to town,
to the harbour,
anywhere with a view.

Out here today
wild horses at the five-bar gate
sore feet   fear   weak legs
that turned around

Out here today
nothing but sky
two lovers
sitting in warm air
looking out
to Skomer.

LENGTH OF DAYS

The nothing of nights has brought me
here once more, to be by your side
with daylight pouring in, the safety of two,
a vegetable life of holding your hand.

How could I take your eyes for granted,
the slate blue, inside of oyster shells,
pearls, the quintessence of you,
something more than flesh and bone?

We need no words for knowing the thunder,
discord in a day's journey. There are moments
on the outside of skin, a ripple of electricity
that shocks us again into the divine,

day and night, the starlight's void,
that irresistible space between you and me.

EATING SPAGHETTI WITH YOU AT 6 PM

is so relaxing, watching you hold your spoon and fork like a prince handling silver and gold cutlery, your chubby fingers orchestrating the plate. I've watched you organise your food, year after year as you settle in comfortably beside me at the table, peas and chips moved to the edge, solitary, waiting in line for the mouth, how precisely you pick each piece of food like a gourmet chef, your art of choice, and I wonder where it all began, was it when you were just a lad gazing out of windows waiting for a father flying high in the sky, off to Africa, Japan, India, Ireland, on a daily trip or a long haul, far away from you and your brother, from safety and joy.

You tell me over and over how good the food is, how you've only learnt to talk about the playground when we are together, how staying at the edge of life has helped you beam when you create cyphers, programme a life away on computers. I show you difference, my wild naked feet on the cold kitchen floor, loud music on the sound bar, Jimi Hendrix or Janis Joplin blaring their hearts out to be heard; but today it's all about the subtle difference between you and me that counts, like those gold stars at school, or how you prefer parmesan on top of your spaghetti and I hunger for the salt in cheddar. Sometimes when we rest, put our spoons down and gaze out across the Tame valley, your blue slate eyes, my green eyes, silence is all we need to soak up the losses we have gathered, that shocking news last week, your darling granddaughter.

LOSS
SOMETHING
ADRIFT
IN TWILIGHT

RAIN FALLING IN MY FACE

Does the weather forecast matter anymore?
All we do now is watch it happen from windows,
peer into clouds that manifest forgotten gods,
think someone on Mount Olympus can save us
from ourselves.

I stand under the showerhead imagine it as rainfall
and wish that I had run naked in a thunderstorm, just once.
I thought I'd told you enough times how much I love you,
but now sunshine only catches the outside of this home.

I only gaze at the moon when my days become nights of
waking to a wrong clock. On days of hurricanes, I press
my palms hard on the glass to feel the vibrations of wind,
pray I will feel it shift through my hair once more,
that my blood will rush to my head with joy.

I dream to be wild with snowfall, feel ice over my skin.
Some days my heart holds onto your soft face here
in the mirror beside me and the arias of you echo in my ears,
birdsong for those few hours each spring.

LOST

I've thought of you
thorn in my heart
scream in my throat
country lanes
rock pools
bare feet on sand
dancing in another year
I've thought about you
our long history of rooms
bedsits on High Lane
your house in a Mill Town
my home full of children
and the lilac tree
outside the front door—
years of visits and stop overs
lost to that hurricane
that tampered with hearts
those days in our kitchens
the woks   the stir fry's
we ate together   now lost—
remember that fairy ring
that appeared overnight
foretelling someone's future
I still hold the rose quartz
you gave me   it wonders
why you couldn't breathe
why your heart thumped so loudly
why you shook with fear
in your bedroom
why I look inside
my small wooden box
to taste the salt of tears
look how they gather
and swim together

AS IF I DIDN'T KNOW THE STORY.

Last night we were
back on holiday
by the dreaming seat
and circle of stones.

That time when you slept
through a lawnmower's roar
outside your window, me knocking,
knocking on your door.

I think about magic,
how every house I choose
is on a ley line. I think about pain
and not understanding your fear.

Last night we walked by
Bosherton Lily ponds,
their white petals and yellow hearts
oblivious to the Sand Martins
whistling over our heads.

As usual I run into the sea
as you sit away from the tide.
Your mouth blows me back
into a cave of alone.

What remains?
A photograph of friends
when we used to laugh
strong as silver birch
sisters of peeling bark.

I must be missing you.

BELTANE 2020

for Diane

It's five am.
Light has crept into my dream and caught me off guard.

And I think of people who have been awake all night
waiting for the moment when this new day begins.
The rituals to be carried out, the night songs,
the dawn songs, the dance of all those flames
being carried into each hearth, the multitude of
small fires banking-in for another year of summer;
this year, a summer like no other, where we mouth the words
but no one hears, where we stand alone on hilltops,
dance in front rooms, remember ribbons around a maypole.

And I think of you in your mill-town valley,
of all those years we laughed, played, walked
to find bluebells, stood in awe of their luminosity.
And I wonder why, in this year of uncertainty,
disappearance of nesting birds, a forest floor's
pungency filled with wild garlic, the preciousness
of each human breath, why we could never gather
enough forgiveness to move beyond such gravel
in our mindsets, fear from our inadequacies.

And I cry on this May Day
without a posy of violets in my hand
to place with love into yours.

LISTENING TO WIND CHIMES IN THE GARDEN 17.4.2020

On days like this when wind shakes chaos over the washing, the towels, sheets and T-shirts, songs are born by metal tubes tuned into their own keys and hearts open up to vibrations in every gust—the aquilegias in full bud dance a tango and rumba, and even though I have the feeling of forgiveness right here in my back yard I can't find the consonants or vowels, or muster the strength to build a fire, fetch a blanket and send you smoke signals into your heaven, I don't have the gift to catch a carrier pigeon with angel's wings and place my letters and cyphers into the metal container, my calm words to let you know I'm fine, I could write an explanation on white paper about misunderstandings, fold it over and over and place it in a glass bottle, but I have no ocean by my side to send it to your far off shores, on days like this when wind shakes chaos into my abandoned heart, songs are born by metal tubes tuned into their own keys and hearts open up to vibrations in every gust, I think I'll write how Time can heal a separation of thoughts and tie my message on a balloon's string, let this gallant wind carry it to you gently today.

FORTUNE TELLING

I knew before I got there as I walked under old oaks and sycamores' their branches weighed down with rain walked past untended graves where only robins and blackbirds sing praises to old bones laying underneath sod after sod of earth that you would be there sitting on a pew being serene and quietly being perfect and that our eyes would meet once more that our history— pages of our lives would turn and turn become kaleidoscope that our dresses of silks and satins days of getting high on hashish on nature itself would live for a moment that you would be there sitting pretty on a pew waiting for the sadness of a lost life carried in a wooden box down the aisle that you would act as if nothing had come between us that we would be young again and sing the song from the prayer book together that all red roses blue iris's and white lilies would see sense in two friends holding hands that the simple act of breathing slowly in and out would be enough to conjure a smile onto a living face

IGLOO

I never built myself an igloo
to understand the inside of ice,
but I know the sharp edges that
slice under the skin.

I know the memory of losing,
burnt images of you on my retina,
as if I had gazed directly
into the sun.

I never built myself an igloo
to hibernate from blizzards,
but I know the avalanches
that covered me
lead-heavy with snow,
unmovable limbs,
the drift with each lover leaving.
The nine-below-zero numbness
in every root of me.

I never built myself an igloo
to cosset my gifts and laughing heart,
but I searched for icebergs and polar winds,
a white bear standing alone.

A single snowflake lands in quiet spaces
and softens the tarmac like the thaw
inside my heart when finally
you touched my palm.

AMULET
MOON IN
THE WATER

WORRY DOLL

Today is cast with all shades of grey
I have no name for a sunless sky
In my palm a worry doll in a rainbow dress
I tell her my sadness about the sun
Will this golden orb soak us in heat
bring lighter skies after supper

Today is Odin and Thor   is a Snow Queen
My palm cradles a worry doll that smiles
Will yellow rays shake the crystal dropper
hanging in the window   bring rainbows on the wall

Today I cannot face a drawn curtain knowing
how near to the edge of whiteouts we are
In my palm a tiny hope of colour
Silently she listens   soaks up my fears

YESTERDAY APRIL 2020

Hours pass by. I'm surfing eBay.
I become numb to my addiction of hoarding.
I finger through the Sahara, Grizas and Out of Xile
silks and linens of my desire.

I only bother with the used items to find a bargain.
I bid for blue velvet trousers and imagine I'm thin again,
dancing to Salif Keita or PJ Harvey.

I instantly buy an embroidered mirror-work dress
from the Sindh. I'll pack it away with my antique textiles
and feel like a pirate with a chest full of treasures.

Something nags at my consumer brain
and I troll the face mask section wondering
which one might save my life. I choose a designer
pink one with black stars printed on the fabric.

I think the colour will go with most of my outfits.
I wonder if I will be able to breathe when I wear it.
This one has no filters.

My son keeps reminding me to buy seeds
and grow my own. I look for carrots, beans and leeks.
I buy wild flowers and a poetry book by Seamus Heaney,
the one with Postscript on the last page.

My son warns me that food will run out, he tells me
to buy tins of beans, tomatoes and salmon. My day
is brightened when I find apple and plum trees for sale.

I buy enough for an orchard and think of all the beauty
I will see when they blossom. I never think about the years
they will take to prosper.

AMULET FOR THE BIGGER PICTURE 26.4.2020

Mine's a fire boulder opal from Queensland, a rock
that speaks to my root chakra, keeps me grounded when
I rub her between my thumb and index finger.

I love her smooth dark surface, a mystery that holds
fire within, a sleeping dragon of opalescent red, blue,
purple and green sparks.

Mine's a magic crystal that feeds my crown chakra.
When she blazes, flecks her rainbow fire at my eyes
I am sky and stars; I am Mars and Venus.

I carry her in my pocket; I cup her in my palm.
I remember when I found her at the holistic fair
in Gorton Monastery years ago.

I had never seen such flames within a solid thing.
I'd never felt the zip-wire move so steadfastly
through my being.

THE NEED FOR TIDES

April 19th 2020

In my museum of daily walks, I found a triangle of green glass,
a pyramid, a jigsaw piece of something that belonged to a whole bottle.

This small piece of green is a script of faraway coastlines lost to April,
May and June, where I could be bare-foot on Bridlington Sands, crazy on
Seaham's treasured shores, naked on Marloe's mile, be gazing at Skomer
from the Deer Park or squinting at Bardsey from the Goddess Stone.

It reminds me of the Aventurine necklace I bought mum
when she told me about her failing heart. The crystal book says
it's good for that chakra. She gave it back when her heart wore out;
she gently placed it in my hands.

A PRAYER FOR FREEDOM 25.4.2020

In the noontime sun I dig, turn the soil over, remove factory bricks, stone and pyramids of sharp glass from forgotten lives. I rake and sift debris from Time and tip out the pot bound hellebores that have been screaming since last summer. I gently prize them out of a plastic prison and place them as if they are my babies being birthed into a new world where worms slither freely, where the idea of stretching out is an unstoppable drug that reaches down to the spring that runs under my house. As the weeks turn to months, I am pot bound, my raison d'etre to climb up and down stairs, window gaze and sunbath in the silence of imaginary beaches and waves, the yearn to go anywhere just a story book. Then I notice the blue-tits arrive outside my kitchen door, inspect the bird box with a manic ritual of pecking heads and tweets and the adventure begins—in front of my eyes, hour after hour, nest building, expectation of new life, at least twenty rose buds, a white (bluebell), and helicopter seeds on the Acer flowers.

SITTING IN A PINK DECKCHAIR NEXT TO MUM AND DAD ON WOOLACOMBE BEACH 1956

It's noon, the sun blazes,
the tide is coming in.
The noise of waves
like medicine or a drug
for anyone around
as we all run blindly into the sea.

Crabs are everywhere, seagulls
with yellow beaks
try to nick ice creams or cheese butties,
mum is smoking, dad ties his hankie
with four knots and covers his head.

It's very hot, we gasp for water.
Dad's skin burns. The sand
is compact enough to build
mansions and moats.

There are no airplanes in the sky.
This is a memory without a care
in the world. If only I'd listened more
to the radio, maybe
I would be famous.

WHEN I WRITE TO YOU,

hope will be in the roses.
I can tell you about their bold blossoms but never
their heady aromas, how each |velvet petal is never wasted.
I collect the dead-heads, gold dust to me, that bring back
a child mulching roses in a jam jar and the belief she had
of making perfume, capture their hypnotic zest forever.

When I sit down with pen and ink,

despair will be under this skin. I can tell you how the outer
layers have changed, how sunshine has bronzed the pink,
how calm resides as illusion in the pores, but never about
the tremors near cartilage and bone, never about blood
that howls under this skin.

When I call out your name each dawn,

love will struggle in her small box of alone. I can tell you
about love's gentle sobbing, how she hates new normal,
but never about the taste of salt, pool of tears she carries
into the garden to water a rose.

When I post my lost world to you, I'll walk away
from these months of cyphers, I'll wonder how
swallows cope with the journey.

DEAD ZONE

There maybe life
even here in the dark,
some kind of slug language,
silver trails that mean
I can't take it,
roar of bear,
long white fangs
that roll over
the other side
of love.

We,
like cave dwellers
constantly hear
the song of water,
dampness that thinks
it's blood keeping
hope alive.

But here we are
once more darling;
bug, beetle,
sickly worm,
stuck so fast
in this numb zone.
What will it take
to release the suction?

FORGETTING

this pandemic world is to walk the length of Whitesands Bay,
listen to the shrill alarms of a flock of twites moving to another
gorse sanctuary.

Forgetting

is a coastal path full of blackberries and late campion, seed heads
and blue skies; is hearing the plea from a cricket in dying grass,
is crying over a dead seal pup on the shoreline.

Forgetting

is gazing over to Ramsey, a yearn to reach St. Justinian's once more,
or find the wild horses on Penmaen Dewi, and wonder why the small
rocks in the Sound are called *The Bitches.*

Forgetting

is to sit in silence on our wooden bench with no thought of next week.
We are in the sun's light and watch oystercatchers and herring gulls
strut over sand and pebbles, watch waves fierce enough to surf.

BEACHCOMBER

I found you, a soft yellow ball on the tide line
saturated with salt water, I squeezed you dry.

I wondered how many small fingers had
wrapped themselves around you,

a minion printed onto the fabric,
on one side a boy wearing a fig leaf,
on the other a girl in a Hawaiian skirt.

I thought about your softball life,
how you had flown through the air,

rolled over sand, rode the surf, felt love
all over your skin, felt sun, wind, water and snow,

so many temperatures over your yellowness,
like custard, you say come on let's play.

With your Cyclops eye you stare out
at this world as if to say, roll me, bat me,

throw me, squeeze me, love me all the way,
love me all the way into the sea.

FINDING A PORCELAIN CUP HANDLE AT JENNY BROWN'S POINT

Here's a broken life hidden between the limestone pavement
and manufactured red building bricks, the left-overs from the lime kiln.

I've found a white cup handle, its dainty curve like the shape of an ear
and the beech trees are shaking off their yellow and orange leaves,
flying like butterflies onto the mudflats, into the sinking landscape.

They were never crying, just moving on;

same as that day mum moved on the hospital air bed;
how her motion fooled us, how we thought she was still with breath.

NEVER QUITE KNOWING MY MOTHER

Sit me on your knee mama,
tell me your stories of tigers
and monkeys, fill me with how
you lived on the edge of jungles.

Cosset me in your arms mummy,
let your Bay of Bengal sing a lullaby,
monsoon, monsoon, monsoon me
into believing someone loved you.

Cradle me in your eyes mother,
let me be your journey across
a continent, across Arabian seas,
kiss me, kiss me once more.

Hold my two hands mama
over all your oceans, weeks,
months, years, water and dry land
between   between   between.

Dance with me mummy like whales
and dolphins, tell me about sweet
smelling balsam, the foothills of
the Himalayas, the cool air.

Rock me fast asleep mama,
let us swim the channel together,
the white cliffs, our Atlantic drifts,
into your sleep hold me again.

CHIFFON AND BROCADE

I see my mother dressed in pale blue chiffon,
puffed out ball gown, silver court shoes,
diamond rings and ruby ear studs, her hair
still light brown, full of curls.

She steps into the night ready to dance
a waltz or two step. She moves away from me
in dreams, so far I cannot smell her skin any more.

I see my mother clothed in a maroon brocade dress,
it clings to her body like love as she flaunts her freckled
face to her audience of dead relatives; she bites a black
rose in her mouth.

She comes so close to me in daylight we tango across
white wooden boards in my home. When I look down
our hands are clasped together, they tremble to the beat
of castanets, they shake our history into our palms,
into our birthmarks and wrinkled skin.

When I look up she's gone into the dark sky's orchestra.

MUM AT THE AIRPORT

dream 4.4.2020

For some unknown reason I'm going to America and mums by my side, we both have suitcases. This is strange as I've not been on holiday with mum since I was a teenager, the time we went to Butlins at Minehead and I hated every minute of it; you can tell if you look at this black and white photo of me, the scowl on my face and the disapproving glance from Aunty Marg and Lotte. But mum's so young in that shot, so beautiful. Because I've never flown anywhere or left this island before it's odd I should be doing it tonight with mum. We are on a bus travelling to London airport and there's a boy freaking out with fear, so someone gives him an injection to put him to sleep and his dad is taking a last drag of his cigarette and he chucks the butt on the floor: of course, I feel outraged at all of this but can do nothing as my mouth won't move.Mum is old and small; she has her hoodie on and another one over it. I ask her where we're going and she tells me New York, and I ask why everyone's dying there. I ask where will we stay, she says she doesn't know. This brings on my anxiety that's been around for weeks, like the weather's uncertainty, the fact that people are dropping like flies, and I'm festering an agoraphobic approach these days. At the airport mum keeps moving so fast I lose her several times as if she's not really here at all and I can't believe her speed as I've only seen her walk slowly; in fact she took her time with everything. I always wondered how she coped losing her mum at the age of three, and being sent to boarding school at five, and how lost she must have been travelling from Kolkata to Eastbourne at eleven. I can't ask her about such things now, it's far too late. I can't find her at the airport, even with her two hoodies on; but I still have her small white handkerchief in my hand, the one with embroidered violets in the corner, and every time I lift it to my nose I can smell her, and I calm down.

IN THESE DAYS OF ISOLATION

I sing to my houseplant, my kaffir lily
that sits quietly on the kitchen windowsill.
I've read about the secret life of plants,
their sensitivities, how they hear everything
we say, the rows between our lips and see
how we hug each other better.

I whisper to my houseplant, my clivia miniata
that's travelled over two hundred miles
from my mum's heart to mine, how I can
still see mum water you for all those years
in her home. How she loved the orange of you.

I stroke my houseplant's leaves, my bush lily,
rid them of dust and dead matter. I tell her how
I carried her to my home and that being together
for all these years is like my mum's smile and
stroking the soft skin on her cheeks.

I gaze at my houseplant's flowers, my natal lily,
her cinnabar petals, her pistils of sex. I breathe in
her delicate perfume, wonder at immaculate timing,
how each spring she brings joy into my nights of losses.
I know she hears me cry when I wash-up, how I miss
the sound of mum's voice in these days of isolation.

HOLDING HANDS WITH DAD

The Aquilegia Vulgaris are in their final curtain call
as the Astrantia Major`s feathery petals loom a magic in the garden.

The white Canterbury bells dong-dong a rapture of June all over
the washed pebbles that have travelled from an Indian shore.

I'm waiting for the terracotta frog sat in his lotus position
to voice the almighty OM around this small plot of heaven,

to ring the tubular chimes set to the one note of E, the E of elation
that may ricochet right into the centre of my heart.

A heart that is a volcano of off-cuts, of off-beats, of tuned-out
harmonies, as my old man lies in a hospital bed with white skin

that frays at the edges, that's lost its embryonic juices, that's in
a wasteland of unknown smiles. I'm in this Eden where a round

painted face is a sun with red ruby lips, a blood orange that watches
a glitter ball stuck in a plant pot full of snapdragons, heads filled
with gossip.

They wait for just two fingers
to release the motion of talk,
the outlandishness of life.

SPIRIT

I'm sitting on the tram, the warm air circulates
and the girls talk, the men are silent, and many
fingers are tapping away, heads down to a machine.

I get this funny feeling, a ghosting of my mum.
She floats above me. How young she is, how happy
she seems and she reaches out her arms to hold me.

I almost believe she's found me, that she's
seen sense in the day she sent me away from home,
but a jerk from the tram pulls me away from dreams.

HER VOICE

silenced
in a swallow's song

her eyes
grey as
hands and feet

she
something solid
in the garden

her mulch of
rose petals

blood like
water

her crying days
under
a
copper beech

secrets from
a child's
perfume

VARANASI

Rolled round the tongue Varanasi is
a sound, a mantra, a beginning and end.

See my Diyas, oil and wick, sacred flame
to my unknown past. I offer you rose petals
my grandmother. See my hands cupped with
water from the Ganga. I lift a memory of you
high to sky, a memory my mother held as a child.

I let you go again as drops fall to the ghats,
bounce from muslin and silk, from all those
pilgrims into mud from the Himalayas,
soil of our ablutions, our daily motions,
a spiritual wondering of home.

Rolled round the tongue Varanasi is
a sound, a mantra, a beginning and end.

A LIGHTNESS IN A GOLDFINCH'S SONG 20.4.2020

Her mind is a fog in the black geranium's flower-head.
The sun warms her naked legs as she sits on the stone seat.
Something in the air has changed; it's easier to breathe
and there's a lightness in a goldfinch's song, their talk
of worms and black Niger seeds, but still her memory
tricks her. She can't reach her ritual of a marriage day,
of something new, something old, something borrowed,
something blue.

The washing dances on the line in today's North wind,
blows through towels, nickers, sheets and dusters,
through her neural pathways, a hurricane through her
blue velvet wedding dress, her embroidered rainbow silks,
it shifts through her long brown hair as she holds her mum's
small white pocket handkerchief, a gift lying in her hand.

She wonders about the Evil Eye,
    has followed her through the years.
    She never wore a blue garter
    or had a sixpence in her left shoe.
    She remembers the white orchard
    pinned to her breast, its sweet perfume,
    and how a day of happy faces
    became a nightmare in the copper beech.

Her mind is a mist in the purple buds of the lilac tree.
Blue-tits visit the feeders like clockwork, they hang
upside down, pendulums in time as they peck
at sunflower seeds, heart of another flower.
She retells a story from her treasure chest,
her days of social distances, when some man
she loved once kept her locked inside for years.

FROM THE BEDROOM WINDOW, NO SIGN OF RAINBOWS, JUST

grey, the pigeons haunt the rooftops.
Copper, about forty-five dry crisp leaves left on the beech tree.
Mulch, dead life covering the pebbles. Yesterday,
I found a dead rat, just its fur and tail, all that's left
after each named storm. The glitter ball hangs
on a bare branch, I can see the sky reflected
within its silver, as far as Carrbrook across the valley,
where the roman road trails to Indian Head at Dove Stone,
where Canada Geese flock, shit by the waterside.

I remember, in our first year of passion,
we walked up to Chew reservoir, almost able to touch the sky,
we saw lapwings nesting, heard their courting songs.
It's a hard walk, a sharp gradient to wild moors,
cotton tops and heather bushes. We saw two women
wild swimming in the rusted iron water, we wondered
how deep, the water, this love.

For a moment today the sun breaks out, drops a ray
on the coming celandines, yellow, bright yellow flakes,
golden, then grey again, pigeons
a nag in the cerebrum, their constant cooing.
The garden is abandoned to fate, which shakes my skin
like a snake sloughing, a tingle up the spine, a shiver
when the radio plays that melody or when
you recite that line in Postscript by Heaney;
how duped we all are about being masters of our fate.
Bloody pigeons, how they haunt my rooftops.

FLOWER MOON*, 24TH APRIL, 2024

Spring is slow in the valley, buds cupped tight
in anticipation of warmth. Violets are here,
tiny purple splashes amongst the depths of green,
a hundred names for shades of beginnings.

Yesterday a Robin came close to the back door,
feeding on invisible things, we looked at each other.
I've tried to imitate Robin talk; they seem to listen.
There are many names for April's full moon,
spawning and goose egg moon are my favourites.

There's no evidence to say why I'm affected,
why sleep is disturbed, why I fly into a rage
or sob unexpectedly, why I seem like someone else;
but oceans become fuller, plump up their tides.
Oysters close their shells, lions hunt in daylight.

* *Cherokee name for April's full moon*

BATHTUB BLUES

Now you're gone into darkness,
like the owl and fox, I search
for any titbit to hold onto.

Today I bring back bath-time,
you and me skinny dipping,
babes in water, oblivious
to this hurting world.

See here,
our yellow ducks
and submarines
our splishy-splashy stories,
our laughter in the tub,
then that noise,
water swirling
down the plug hole,
years passing,
our small shrivelled fingertips
from staying too long in water.

Thank the stars
for mum's love,
see her wrap us up
in warm towels
all that rub a dub,
the butcher
the baker
the candlestick maker malarky.

Oh, bloody hell bro,
your cheeky smile,
your golden hair,
this rift in my heart.

BLOSSOM

From the depths,
these days of threats,
the purest white
of blackthorn flowers
fallen to
towpath and hedgerow,
today surrounded by
concrete road and path
the Japanese cherry
in full bloom
melted this heart,
the shock of pink
against grey
brought back faith
for the simple things
a season's regularity
comfort in petals
pistils stamens pollen
sepal ovule stigma
ovary anther
a bee's song a bees hum
in Japan the flowers
are known as Sakura
and the ritual
of viewing the spectacle
of spring arriving
is Hanami
a thing of beauty
lasting only weeks
transient beings
a message from
the blossom
for our short lives.

THINKING ABOUT THE ENDING,

not in a storybook sense, but the reality of where to scatter our ashes. Years ago, when I was on my own, I chose Culbone church in the middle of nowhere just past Porlock Weir, by the grass cuttings and brook, by the leper's window: it's still a favourite place of mine. Then, when we found love, we picked that place on the edge of the land by Eglwys, Llanbadrig, where the sea is wild, we wanted the sea and white horses. This year when our bones and minds are becoming ridiculous, when time has captured you and me following our lost loves across to Avalon, we thought about who would scatter us and how far they might travel to let us go, we thought about you letting me go, we thought about me letting you go. You told me about scattering your mum and dad, how you'd kept your mums ashes safely to be with your dad and then let them fly on Pwllheli beach near the golf clubhouse, how that was a huge thing. I told you I hated that my mum and dad were under stone slabs, not even together, just side by side on some vast hillside where no one passed by. We nod at each other, stare into tonight's cloudless sky, Venus and Orion's Belt so bright we almost believe in an afterlife. We put our pens down, leave the decision for now, go back into that trance, you know don't you, avoidance technique, we plan another holiday in Laugharne, to go to our favourite place, by the boat planted with yellow irises and red poppies, where we sit and gaze out at the mud flats, watch the heron's patience and the Taf coming in and out.

WALKING BESIDE THE SHINE OF SILVER BIRCH AND GOLD FINCH SONGS

my left eye only catching the blur,
my right eye compensating for soft birch bark peeling off,
for ash trees swishing in the breeze, some comfort
for the leaving of sight, the soft bark like a baby's skin.
To go back would be no good. To think the bluebells in April,
my maroon penstemon or the violets tucked into stone and pebble,
to think such beauty like the lilac I planted
ten years ago, in the back yard, could suss out my grief
of losing such a thing as sight. These days I practise in the dark,
from bed to bathroom, picking up small things from the table,
medicine, water in a cup, my dreaming crystal, my lavender oil,

the dying of the light, the dying of the light.

Yesterday, I sat in sunshine between birch trees and rain puddles,
mud under my shoes, worms wrestling with themselves.
I watched goldfinches come again to the feeder, come again
to the niger seeds. I listened to their song, a song I cannot
sing to you. I cannot get the trill of such a tiny pitch.
I lost myself in their small throats as if I belong to their song,
my spine bent double as I dance to the music of arias,
of a finch chorus, as if I had come again to flock,
that idea of being more than one, a gathering of sight and song.

I gathered beech nuts spread over pebbles.
I was blackbird and sparrow, even starling in the garden,
such a mouth full of song, such eyes fading with the light,
look how I fill my loss with song
gold of finch, golden wings,

the dying of the light, the dying of the light.

THE DEATH TREE

St Michael's Church, Laugharne

I whisper to the death tree, ask for some of her red bark–
a talisman to keep in my pocket.

I crave silence. She knows about perseverance–
lets her branches grow into the earth.

I pull gently and she lets some go into my world from hers–
she knows about other worlds,

the dark and light of days, the past and present.

She's toxic, every berry and seed can conjure
life or death.

I whisper to the death tree, she gives me hope–
like an angel's wings
to give me flight
to give me flight.

ACKNOWLEDGEMENTS

Thank you to Mark Davidson,
for his faith in my work and his
positive verve for publishing poetry.

Thank you to all my family,
especially my partner and best friend
Keith Lander who listens to all my poems!

Thanks to my 3 sons,
Stephen, Mark and Gavin,
who cringe when I mention poetry:
but without them
I would be a lesser human being.

Thank you to all the poets I have met
along my journey, there are many
who have inspired my work,
workshopped my words,
helped me to believe in myself.

www.ingramcontent.com/pod-product-compliance
Lightning Source LLC
Chambersburg PA
CBHW050442200726
48295CB00024B/951

9781916830356